JESUS ALONE

The Story of the Savior

Jerry Mattix

To our three children, Ishael, Tirzah and Gabriel.

Stay close to Jesus.

And after six days Jesus took with him Peter and James, and John his brother, and led them up a high mountain by themselves. And he was transfigured before them, and his face shone like the sun, and his clothes became white as light. And behold, there appeared to them Moses and Elijah, talking with him. And Peter said to Jesus, "Lord, it is good that we are here. If you wish, I will make three tents here, one for you and one for Moses and one for Elijah." He was still speaking when, behold, a bright cloud overshadowed them, and a voice from the cloud said, "This is my beloved Son, with whom I am well pleased; listen to him." When the disciples heard this, they fell on their faces and were terrified. But Jesus came and touched them, saying, "Rise, and have no fear." And when they lifted up their eyes, they saw no one but Jesus only.

MATTHEW 17:1-8

CONTENTS

JESUS ALONE

INTRODUCTION

I f we were to travel down the dusty corridors of time and peer into the hall of fame of mankind we would see many familiar names of men and women who have left indelible marks on human history. Some of these have etched themselves onto mankind's collective memory by accomplishing heroic feats on the battlefield, others by leaving for posterity literary masterpieces as a tribute to their intellectual brilliance. However there is one person who has impacted more people across the globe than any other and this without ever lifting a sword or even wielding a pen. In fact, he left no great works to his name and yet more literary works have been written about him than any other human in history.

Despite living a humble and relatively short life in a remote corner of the Roman Empire, Jesus' life and teachings have served to inspire more positive change over the last two millennia than any other human being. Although most are familiar with his name, an increasing number of people are strangers to what he really embodied. Even though much of what we treasure in our modern world —freedom and equality—can be traced directly to him, the man himself has been covered in layers of religious traditions and shrouded in mystery. Sadly, most have grown used to hearing Jesus' name solely as a swear word in Hollywood movies or in pop songs. Still, he stands alone, truly unique and unrivaled in his tremendous impact on human history. It is time to revisit the origins of this timeless enigma. It is time to meet the real Jesus.

Most have an opinion about who they think Jesus Christ was; for some he was a prophet, for others a wise sage and yet for others he was none other than the Son of God. In the modern world, where, despite the unprecedented proliferation of knowledge, conjecture and conspiracy theories run rampant, so much so that people are wary of staking a claim in anything called truth. This sad state of affairs hinders most people from accepting anyone's opinion about anything, especially when it comes to religious matters. However when it comes to ascertaining the truth about the life and teaching of Jesus Christ, we are not restricted to certain people's point of views or interpretations; rather we can each read the Bible for ourselves. While some have grown accustomed to dismissing the Bible as an archaic book full of fables, the fact is that no other book in human history has proven itself so reliable time and again.

For those not familiar with the Bible, it is

divided into two sections: Old and New Testaments. The Old Testament begins with the creation and fall of humankind and goes on to chronicle God's dealings with the nation of Israel. His stated purpose is to bless all nations and redeem all peoples by revealing himself through his chosen people. This master plan of salvation comes to fruition in the New Testament where Jesus, the long-awaited Savior, begins to fulfill all of God's promises.

The New Testament begins with four accounts of the life of Jesus called the Gospels. This is followed with a short history of the early church in the book of Acts and a number of letters written to first century church fellowships and individuals with instruction on Christian theology and practical living. All of these are capped with the book of Revelation in which the risen Jesus himself reappears to the apostle John and reveals things yet future.

In order to truly appreciate the facts about the life and teaching of Jesus Christ we must turn our attention to the original eyewitness accounts as recorded in the Bible. Much speculation has been made about who Jesus really was, however any interpretive theories that refuse to honestly engage the Biblical text, not only do us all a disservice, but also result in further propagating disinformation. In short, if we are genuinely sincere in our desire to uncover the real Jesus, we must begin our query in the most ancient account of his life, the Gospels.

That being said, we should also be aware of the intensely personal and spiritual nature of this quest. This is because, according to the Bible, Jesus rose from the grave and is alive. To this day, many testify to his miraculous intervention in their lives in response to their prayers. Thus, in our search for him, we shouldn't be surprised to find that he was actually searching for us all along.

Now a word on why I felt compelled to write this book. As noted earlier, myriads of books have been written on the person and teachings of Jesus Christ; why another? First of all, there seems to be a growing disconnect between those who were raised hearing all about Jesus in Sunday School, who are intimately acquainted with all the details of his life, and the growing majority of people in the world who have only ever heard his name used as a byword. Thus we cannot go on assuming that everyone knows what we are talking about when we speak of Jesus the Nazarene. Secondly, as a Bible teacher I am regularly accosted with questions about Christianity, most of which begin something like this: "Why do Christians do....?" or "What does Christianity teach about...?" These are all valid questions but I am often struck with how most of them focus on the theological teachings or history of Christianity instead of on the actual person of Jesus Christ.

Many books have been written explaining Christian history and answering questions pertinent to our beliefs and practices. Seeking to decipher the development of Christian dogma down through history is both an exhausting and exciting challenge but it ultimately takes us away from the heart of the matter, namely Jesus. The fact is that there would be no Christianity without Jesus Christ. Consequently, whatever our opinion of the evolution of Christianity over the last two millennia and its many modern representations, including the strange behavior of some of its adherents, we must first start by understanding Jesus and then judging all later developments against the backdrop of his person and teachings.

We all naturally tend to judge a book by its cover. Thus we judge Christianity based on what we see in the lives of Christians we have seen. We likewise judge Islam based on the news coming from the Middle East, just like we judge Hindus based on movies from Bollywood. So we conclude that all Hindus worship cows, that all Muslims are terrorists and that all Christians are hypocrites.

Now anyone with a slight bit of sense can see the nonsense of these simplistic and prejudiced conclusions. Simple logic would tell us that any fair analysis of a religion or ideology must start with its point of inception. And yet, in an age when we have more information at our fingertips than ever before, we still tend towards intellectual laziness. In short, an unbiased critique of Christianity should first and foremost focus on the person of Christ and the teachings of Jesus.

In this book my hope is to take you back to

the heart of Christianity, to meet the person of Jesus Christ. Just like his original followers sought to express in writing the amazing truths they witnessed to their generation, I hope to take those same historical facts and make them understandable to our generation. I would only ask that for now you put aside whatever has been your experience with or preconceived notions about Christianity and take an honest look at the person of Jesus. The fact that this one man has singlehandedly impacted the world more than any other human being deserves our attention. Despite all that has been attributed to his name since the time he walked on this earth two thousand years ago, there is no questioning the fact that Jesus was and continues to be the single most inspiring and influential person in human history. Why is that? His life surely deserves a second look. Now please allow me to introduce you to the real Jesus of the Bible...

THE PROMISED ONE

A normal person's life begins with his or her birth. However, from the outset Jesus' life is unique in that long before he was born in Bethlehem many clear and specific predictions pertinent to his life and ministry were recorded in the Old Testament. Centuries in advance prophets spoke of his imminent arrival. In fact, from the very dawn of time his life is intricately and inextricably woven into the whole fabric of human history. Let's start at the beginning of mankind's story.

The Bible opens with an elegant description of how God created everything from nothing in six days. After the first day, he especially focused his creative wisdom and power on our planet, organizing and minutely calibrating all the diverse components of our existence in order to sustain life on the earth. Then on the final day of creation he created humans and placed them in charge of this new world. The Bible stresses that humans are uniquely created *"in his image"*, that is to say that we bear God's "spiritual DNA." The implications of this magnificent truth for all of us are truly amazing. This means that humans were created as God's spiritual offspring and were intended to live in intimate relationship with him.

Later we read that in this new world, God planted a gorgeous garden called Eden, where Adam and Eve were to live in complete harmony with creation and their Creator. However in this new arrangement, unlike the other living creatures on the planet, humans were spiritual beings equipped with a free will. Thus, even though they were placed in a perfect world, from the outset God warned them that rebellion against the established order, in the form of eating from the forbidden tree, would result in fatal consequences. In this way their love and loyalty to the Creator was to be tested. Ultimately God would not force them to reciprocate his love; they had to choose to do so by trusting in his goodness and obeying his command.

Soon afterward, Adam and Eve were approached by a talking serpent, apparently possessed by Satan, a fallen angel who had rebelled against God. He slyly engaged Eve in conversation and began to sow seeds of doubt in her heart. Satan went on to challenge God's stated command and urge humans to take charge of their own fate. Sadly, instead of choosing to trust in their loving Creator, Adam and Eve fell for the devil's lies.

As soon as they ate from the forbidden tree they felt deep shame and recognized the dreadful mistake they had made. However when confronted by God, instead of seeking his forgiveness they compounded their guilt by passing the blame and making excuses for their rebellion. In this way our ancestors were infected with sin and this deadly contagion ultimately spread to all humans.

It is at this critical juncture in human history we find the first allusion to Jesus. Even as God was detailing for Adam and Eve the tragic consequences of their rebellion, including pain in childbirth and ruptured marriage relationships, he also spoke directly to Satan, saying: *"I will put enmity between you and the woman, and between your offspring and her offspring; he shall bruise your head, and you shall bruise his heel" (Genesis 3:15).* These words are a declaration of war. It seems that Satan, by luring humans into his rebellion, was hoping they would be his for good. God however, refused to surrender his spiritual children to the devil's schemes and instead drew the battle lines between them. He particularly highlighted *"the offspring of the woman"* one who would crush the serpent in a yet future epic encounter.

This cryptic phrase *"the offspring of the woman"* is rich with meaning and mystery. Who is this great champion who will one day defeat the devil? Why is he strangely described as the offspring or seed of the woman? Finally, in crushing the serpent why is he also seen as being bruised or bitten by the same? From ancient times many scholars saw in this passage the first clue to the coming of Jesus the Messiah. Against the backdrop of humanity's disastrous fall into sin, the hope of a Savior was welcome news indeed.

After Adam and Eve were expelled from the Garden of Eden they were soon confronted with the tragic results of their sin when Cain, their firstborn son, murdered his own brother Abel. From then on the family line of Cain spiraled out of control with one of his descendants boasting about his marrying multiple women and killing a man in cold blood. During this period of history mankind became so utterly depraved that *every imagination of the thoughts of his heart was only evil continually* (Genesis 6:5). Furthermore, they somehow managed to engage demonic spirits so that the human race was polluted beyond repair. In the end God chose to expunge all evil from the face of the earth with a global flood. However he also had a promise to keep: the promise of the *offspring of the woman.*

At this time God chose to save Noah and his family from the impending judgment. He had Noah build a massive boat large enough to hold a representative sampling of all animal species on earth. Later, when the flood waters covered the planet, Noah and his floating zoo were spared God's wrath. Afterwards, Noah's children and the animals began to populate the earth once more but it didn't take long for the effects of sin and moral corruption to resurface. Soon humans once again banded together in rebellion against God. This is vividly illustrated in their construction of the tower of Babel whereby humans outright challenged God's authority by building a towering pagan Temple to exalt themselves. However, before they were able to finish the structure, God confused their languages and scattered mankind to the four corners of the earth.

Time and again mankind had shown itself incapable of living in harmony with God and his good world. They continued to rebel against God's commands but he would not allow his righteous purposes to be thwarted. This time he chose Abraham and made a covenant with him that echoed the promise of the "*offspring*" made earlier to Adam and Eve. God called Abraham to leave behind the corruption of Babel and follow his lead to a new land where God would bless him with offspring as numerous as the stars in the sky. He further told him that his "*offspring*" would become a blessing to all the nations of the world. In time God miraculously blessed Abraham with many descendants. These later settled in the land of Egypt where they awaited the fulfillment of God's promises to Abraham.

Years went by and the offspring of Abraham multiplied even as they hung on to the promise of a Savior. By now they had become slaves of a cruel Pharaoh, but God remembered his covenant and raised up Moses to miraculously deliver his people from bondage. Once free from Pharaoh, they all gathered around Mount Sinai to hear God's commands. He invited them to make a covenant with him whereby they would become the model nation for all mankind. Despite initially agreeing to God's terms, the Israelites soon fell into gross idolatry and moral perversion. In fact, the rest of the history of Israel, as chronicled in the Old Testament, is a sad litany of their failure in the face of God's great faithfulness.

It was in this context that God repeatedly sent prophets to warn his people of impending judgment but also to continue to pave the way for the promised Savior. Moses, the first great leader of the nation of Israel, explicitly spoke of him saying: *"The LORD your God will raise up for you a prophet like me from among you, from your brothers, it is to him you shall listen"* (Deuteronomy 18:15). Moses recognized the hopelessly stubborn nature of the people and knew that they ultimately needed someone even greater than himself to lead them back into a harmonious relationship with God. He specified that this Savior would come from the nation of Israel.

In succeeding years God, through the prophets, further delineated the profile of the promised *"offspring"* who would crush the serpent and bring blessing to all mankind. Let's look at a few of their prophecies:

- Micah 5:2 (700 BC) - *"But you, O Bethlehem Eph-rathah, who are too little to be among the clans of Judah, from you shall come forth for me one who is to be ruler in Israel, whose coming forth is from of old, from ancient days."* - The prophets had predicted that the promised Savior would come from the tribe of Judah. The prophet Micah further speci-fied that he would be born in the otherwise in-significant town of Bethlehem. However he also noted that the true source of this promised one could be traced back long before his birth.

- Isaiah 7:14 (700 BC) - *"Therefore the Lord himself will give you a sign. Behold, the virgin shall conceive and bear a son, and shall call his name Immanuel."* - Centuries before the birth of Jesus the prophet Isaiah spoke of one who would be born of a vir-gin. He further described him by the title *"Imman-uel"* which means, God is with us. In the following chapters he went on to give more details about this miracle child.

- Isaiah 9:5-6 (700 BC) - *"For to us a child is born, to us a son is given; and the government shall be upon his shoulder, and his name shall be called Wonderful Counselor, Mighty God, Everlasting Father, Prince of Peace. Of the increase of his government and of peace there will be no end, on the throne of David and over his kingdom, to establish it and to uphold it with just-ice and with righteousness from this time forth and forevermore."* - The lofty titles showered upon this child are quite remarkable: *Wonderful Counselor,*

Mighty God, Everlasting Father, Prince of Peace. He is clearly more than just a typical king. These must be interpreted in light of the fact that he is evidently chosen to be the everlasting king to sit on the throne of David. This takes us back even further to the prophecies given to King David.

- 2 Samuel 7:12-14 (1000 BC) - *"When your days are fulfilled and you lie down with your fathers, I will raise up your offspring after you, who shall come from your body, and I will establish his kingdom. He shall build a house for my name, and I will establish the throne of his kingdom forever. I will be to him a father, and he shall be to me a son."* - Like Eve and Abraham, David received the promise of the holy *"offspring"*. God promised David that his dynasty would continue until it was crowned by the coming of the eternal king. This promised one is further described as *"the Son of God."*

- Zechariah 9:9 (500 BC) - *"Shout aloud, O daughter of Jerusalem! Behold, your king is coming to you; righteous and having salvation is he, humble and mounted on a donkey, on a colt, the foal of a donkey."* - The prophet Zechariah made it clear that the promised King would be radically different from what people usually expect from a king. Instead of being arrogant and ostentatious he would be known for his love of righteousness, his healing powers and more than anything his humility. However the greatest surprise is that this Savior and King would be so humble as to actually lay down his life for his subjects.

• Isaiah 53:2-11 (700 BC) - *"For he grew up before him like a young plant, and like a root out of dry ground; he had no form or majesty that we should look at him, and no beauty that we should desire him. He was despised and rejected by men, a man of sorrows and acquainted with grief; and as one from whom men hide their faces he was despised, and we esteemed him not. Surely he has borne our griefs and carried our sorrows; yet we esteemed him stricken, smitten by God, and afflicted. But he was pierced for our transgressions; he was crushed for our iniquities; upon him was the chastisement that brought us peace, and with his wounds we are healed. All we like sheep have gone astray; we have turned—every one— to his own way; and the LORD has laid on him the iniquity of us all. He was oppressed, and he was afflicted, yet he opened not his mouth; like a lamb that is led to the slaughter, and like a sheep that before its shearers is silent, so he opened not his mouth. By oppression and judgment he was taken away; and as for his generation, who considered that he was cut off out of the land of the living, stricken for the transgression of my people? And they made his grave with the wicked and with a rich man in his death, although he had done no violence, and there was no deceit in his mouth. Yet it was the will of the LORD to crush him; he has put him to grief; when his soul makes an offering for guilt, he shall see his offspring; he shall prolong his days; the will of the LORD shall prosper in his hand. Out of the anguish of his soul he shall see and be satisfied; by his knowledge shall the righteous one, my servant, make many to be accounted righteous, and he shall bear their iniquities."* - These lines, written many centuries before his birth, clearly spell out the suffering of Jesus on the cross. The promised Savior is portrayed as sacrificing his life for the sake of rebellious mankind. But how could such cruel suffering and ignominious death bring about salvation for mankind? How would he succeed in crushing the serpent even as he himself was being crushed?

Although shrouded in mystery it is abundantly clear that all the critical elements of the life and work of Jesus were spelled out in remarkable detail long before he was born to Mary. Who but God could predict so perfectly such a unique life? Jesus' objective was ordained long ago, his course was charted from the beginning; no mere mortal could possibly fit this mold.

In seeking to understand the person and purpose of Jesus it is essential to recognize his role in the greater purpose of God for mankind. While many still try to claim that he was merely a great teacher or prophet, the fact that the prophets singled him out as the culmination of God's promises makes it impossible to accept Jesus as a mere human.

It is true that he spoke for God, like many other prophets, but Jesus is further described as the very Word of God. Unlike the other prophets that sought God's forgiveness for their sins and failures, Jesus alone appears as the sinless substitute for all mankind. Even the greatest prophets at times fell prey to Satan's temptations but only Jesus succeeded in crushing the devil at the cross. In the end all the prophets passed away but only Jesus rose again victorious over death. But let's not get too far ahead of ourselves...

THE REAL STORY
OF CHRISTMAS

For most, the mention of Christmas conjures up fond memories of family reunions, colorfully wrapped gifts and a scrumptious holiday feast. Today this jolly season is often characterized by the likes of Santa Claus who, with a twinkle in his eye and a bundle of presents in tow, cruises around the globe in his sled pulled by reindeer. However, in all the holiday hustle and bustle, most have lost sight of the real meaning behind Christmas. It is actually a birthday party, but ironically most have forgotten all about the birthday boy, namely Jesus. How is it that his humble birth has inspired such a treasure trove of traditions now celebrated around the globe? To understand this we must go back two thousand years to the events surrounding the birth of Jesus.

Actually, from beginning to end the story

of Jesus' birth is filled with irony. In the centuries leading up to his birth the prophets had laid out for the Jewish people numerous signs of his coming and still they were completely caught by surprise. This happened largely because of their misguided expectations in which they envisioned the promised Savior coming only to fulfill their nationalistic aspirations. They failed to appreciate the deeper meaning and greater purposes in God's master plan.

In all fairness, had we been a Jew awaiting the promised Savior in the first century while suffering under the cruel yoke of Roman rule, like most others, we would have likely fallen prey to such misguided illusions. We might have dreamed of the promised King, the *Messiah,* as he was known by the Jews, appearing out of thin air and leading an army of angels against the enemy. But that was not to be; Jesus' arrival was much more down to earth.

Instead of a wealthy pedigree, his mother and father were humble peasants far from home and forced to give birth to their firstborn in a stable. The first to come and celebrate his birth were not the religious elite but rather meek shepherds from nearby fields. Later he was visited by the Magi from the far east instead of the leaders of his own people. Such were the ironic circumstances surrounding the most famous birth in human history.

It all started with the angel Gabriel paying a visit to a young Jewish maiden name Mary. She had recently become engaged to an honest local craftsman named Joseph and they were undoubtedly

JERRY MATTIX

planning a hearty family wedding celebration, all
the while dreaming about their new life together.
Then an unexpected angelic visit turned everything upside down.

> *Greetings, O favored one, the Lord is with you! Do*
> *not be afraid, Mary, for you have found favor with*
> *God. And behold, you will conceive in your womb*
> *and bear a son, and you shall call his name Jesus. He*
> *will be great and will be called the Son of the Most*
> *High. And the Lord God will give to him the throne*
> *of his father David, and he will reign over the house*
> *of Jacob forever, and of his kingdom there will be no*
> *end (Luke 1:28-33).*

This was a momentous occasion because the
Jews had been longing and waiting for the coming
of the Messiah for centuries. It would be a tremendous honor for Mary to give birth to him. Not only
that, but he was to become the eternal King promised long ago to David. However, she also quickly
realized the human impossibility involved, namely,
that she was a virgin! How could this be? The angel
went on to explain.

> *The Holy Spirit will come upon you, and the power*
> *of the Most High will overshadow you; therefore the*
> *child to be born will be called holy—the Son of God*
> *(Luke 1:35).*

Gabriel explained that because this child
would be born by direct divine intervention he
would not be the average child, he would in fact be

the very Son of God! This was critical because it fulfilled the promise made long ago to Eve about the
Savior being the *"offspring of the woman"*, namely
born of a virgin. It also fulfilled the words spoken
to King David about the eternal king coming from
his family line but actually being the Son of God.
However, as exhilarating as all this was for Mary, she
likely soon began to wonder about how others, especially Joseph, would respond to this news.

Mary was right to worry about this, as pregnancy out of wedlock at that time was punishable
by death. Who would believe such a story? How
would Joseph respond? He responded as anyone else
would, with shock and disbelief. But, he truly cared
for Mary, so he chose to break their marriage en-
gagement quietly, in order to protect her from legal
repercussions. However, around this time, he also
received an angelic visit:

Joseph, son of David, do not fear to take Mary as
your wife, for that which is conceived in her is
from the Holy Spirit. She will bear a son, and you
shall call his name Jesus, for he will save his people
from their sins (Matthew 1:20-21).

In this way Joseph received divine confirm-
ation that collaborated Mary's account. He was
likewise told that the baby's name would be
"Jesus" (Yeshua in his native tongue) which means
"Savior". The gospel record also notes the import-
ance of Jesus being from the family of Abraham and
more specifically from the line of King David. Not

just anyone could lay claim to the title of *Messiah*. In this way we can see that Jesus was uniquely qualified to fulfill the historic role of Savior promised by the prophets long before.

In accordance with the instruction of Gabriel, Joseph did take Mary as his wife. Naturally this also meant shouldering all the slanderous allegations surrounding her unexpected pregnancy. But then came another surprise; the Roman Emperor Caesar Augustus decided to hold a census. Everyone would need to return to the town of his birth in order to be registered. This meant that Joseph and Mary must travel roughly 150 kilometers south to Bethlehem. This was no small feat, especially with a near term pregnancy. However, it did serve to fulfill the prophecy made by Micah about the future Messiah being born in Bethlehem, the birthplace of King David.

Once they arrived in Bethlehem Joseph and Mary naturally expected to be taken in by some family members, as they were originally from that town. However with any number of relatives converging on this small hamlet for the census, there was just no place left for them. The news of her surprise pregnancy may have also made family members less hospitable. Consequently when the time came for her to give birth they were rooming with the farm animals and had little choice but to put the newborn Jesus in the manger or feeding trough.

Surely by now Mary and Joseph were wondering if they had truly gotten the story straight from Gabriel. Was this really the Savior of mankind? How could the Messiah be subjected to such an ignoble birth? Even as they wrestled with such questions, in a nearby hillside, an angel appeared to a group of shepherds tending their flocks.

> *Fear not, for behold, I bring you good news of great joy that will be for all the people. For unto you is born this day in the city of David a Savior, who is Christ (Messiah) the Lord. And this will be a sign for you: you will find a baby wrapped in swaddling cloths and lying in a manger (Luke 2:10-12).*

Initially frightened by the angel, the shepherd wondered why they had been selected to be the first recipients of such momentous news. Like all good Jews, they also were expectantly awaiting the arrival of the promised Messiah. Upon hearing the angel they may have been surprised to hear that the promised Savior was actually the *Lord* himself. This was coupled with the news that they were to find this newborn King not in a palace but in a manger. Suddenly they found themselves surrounded by a host of angels all praising God and saying: *"Glory to God in the highest, and on earth peace among those with whom he is pleased!"*

Hardly believing their ears, they set out to confirm the news of the newborn Messiah. Soon they found themselves in that most unlikely scene described by the angel: *"a baby wrapped in swaddling cloths and lying in a manger."* Mary and Joseph were surely surprised by the unexpected visitors and

23

even more so by their tale of encountering a choir of angels. Their message wonderfully confirmed all that the angel Gabriel had told them months before. Indeed this baby was the promised Savior and King, the very Son of God.

A few days later Mary and Joseph took baby Jesus to the nearby capital city, Jerusalem, where they offered the customary sacrifice at the Temple. Once there they were met by an old man named Simeon. Years earlier he had been told by God's Spirit that he would not die until he saw the awaited Messiah. So upon recognizing the child as the fulfillment of God's promises he exclaimed: *"Lord, now you are letting your servant depart in peace, according to your word; for my eyes have seen your salvation that you have prepared in the presence of all peoples, a light for revelation to the Gentiles, and for glory to your people Israel" (Luke 2:29-32).*

Simeon went on to warn Mary that the life and ministry of Jesus would stir things up politically and would lead to great pain for her personally. Soon afterwards they were approached by yet another person, this time a widow and prophetess named Anna. She also testified to the fact that Jesus was the expected Savior of all people. These encounters were a great shock to Mary and Joseph but also a stark reminder that while the political and religious leaders of the Jews were oblivious to the fulfilled promise, God was confirming his plan to them using his humble servants.

There is one more piece of irony to add to

the puzzle of Jesus' birth. This relates to the most unusual visit of the Magi from the East. These wise men were famous for their knowledge of astronomy and had a long and prestigious history as royal priests and advisors to the Babylonian, Parthian and Greek Kings. So when this renowned group of sages suddenly showed up in Jerusalem, asking about the birth of the Jewish king, it caused quite a stir. The aging and paranoiac king of the Jews, Herod the Great, was especially alarmed. Calling the Magi in for an audience, he inquired about this star they claimed to be following. Clearly he saw the fulfillment of this promised Messiah as a great threat to his reign.

The exact nature of the heavenly sign these wise men witnessed remains a mystery, but the very fact that they knew to look for the great king among the Jewish people, is likely traceable to their interaction with the prophet Daniel. Six centuries earlier Daniel and a group of young Jewish elite were exiled to Babylon by King Nebuchadnezzar. Once there, they were pressed into the service of the king. After a series of remarkable events, whereby Daniel proved his faithfulness to God and interpreted the King's dreams, he was promoted to become head of the King's advisors, the Magi.

Daniel went on to receive a number of prophetic revelations about the rise and fall of worldly kingdoms and the yet future Kingdom of God. He was also visited by the angel Gabriel who gave him an amazingly detailed description of Israel's future, culminating in the coming of the Messiah. In this prophetic masterpiece the angel delineated for Daniel a series of events including the number of years that would transpire leading up to the arrival of the Messiah (See: Daniel 9).

In all likelihood, the Magi were privy to the prophetic writings of Daniel and thus had a good idea of when and where to look for the promised king who would inaugurate God's Kingdom for all mankind. This, combined with some celestial phenomena, spurred them on to the capital city of the Jews, where they began inquiring of the birth of the great king. Ironically the political leaders of the day knew nothing of the matter.

Upon hearing their story Herod inquired from his own advisors and religious leaders as to the location where the promised Messiah was to be born. Once they ascertained that it was Bethlehem, the city of David, Herod sent them on their way, roughly 10 kilometers south, to the hamlet of David. Finding the place where Mary and Joseph resided, they were overwhelmed with joy. To the great bewilderment of his parents, they showered Jesus with gifts worthy of a king: gold, frankincense and myrrh. Then being warned of Herod's evil intent toward the child they left to their own land by another route. Incited by jealousy, Herod was plotting to kill the newborn king, but the angel again warned Joseph and they fled to Egypt.

From the angelic visits to the Magi from the east, the circumstances surrounding the birth of

Jesus are truly unique. This is the true story that inspired the Christmas narrative and continues to fill Christian worshipers with awe and wonder every year. But it is not just the fairy-tale like conditions of the story that give it staying power, it is the fact that it really, truly happened. Furthermore, what these events begin to tell us about the identity of Jesus is indeed awe inspiring. From the outset it was clear that he was born to fulfill a divine calling. He was no mere son of Adam, but rather the promised *"offspring"* of Eve; he came to restore mankind and fulfill the hopes and dreams of all creation.

THE VOICE
IN THE
WILDERNESS

You can always tell when an important politician or famous personality is about to arrive in town. Preparations begin weeks in advance with posters put up, banners flying, hotels decked out and fancy restaurants booked. However, in the case of Jesus, despite his arrival having been predicted by prophets and his birth proclaimed by angels well in advance, there was no real fanfare surrounding his coming. No red carpet, no cocktail parties, no fancy hotel rooms. On the contrary he was placed in a germ-infested manger and welcomed by a band of village shepherds.

The message was abundantly clear, namely, that Jesus was not interested in putting on airs or catching the eye of the elite. He was here for the humble and the meek. But don't let the simplicity of his arrival fool you into thinking that it was not well thought out. Quite the opposite, this was all part of an elaborate plan of salvation for all mankind.

As we saw previously, centuries before his birth prophets spoke in great detail of his coming. They also spoke of one who would come before him to prepare the way. He was described as *"The voice in the wilderness."* His task would be to prepare the hearts of the people to welcome the coming Savior. This was because the Messiah, more than a glittering welcoming committee, desired sincere hearts to greet him upon arrival. So it was that several months before coming to Mary, the angel Gabriel visited someone else in Israel.

Zechariah was a humble man of God serving as a priest in the Temple of Jerusalem. He had been selected by lot to burn incense before the presence of God, a rare privilege for the common priest like him. While the rest of his division was praying outside, expectantly awaiting his reemergence from the Temple, the angel Gabriel suddenly appeared to Zechariah saying:

> *Do not be afraid, Zechariah, for your prayer has been heard, and your wife Elizabeth will bear you a son, and you shall call his name John. And you will have joy and gladness, and many will rejoice at his birth, for he will be great before the Lord. And he*

*must not drink wine or strong drink, and he will be
filled with the Holy Spirit, even from his mother's
womb. And he will turn many of the children of Israel to the Lord their God, and he will go before him
in the spirit and power of Elijah, to turn the hearts
of the fathers to the children, and the disobedient to
the wisdom of the just, to make ready for the Lord a
people prepared (Luke 1:13-17).*

This was welcome news to the old man in
more than one way. Firstly, Zechariah and his wife
Elizabeth had not been able to have a child and were
now quite advanced in years. Secondly, as a priest he
knew of the promise of the forerunner to the Messiah, who was described as *"Elijah"* by the prophet
Malachi. Still, the words of Gabriel seemed too good
to be true. Overwhelmed by the news, Zechariah
went on to question the veracity of the angel's pro-
nouncement, to which he responded:

*I am Gabriel. I stand in the presence of God, and I
was sent to speak to you and to bring you this good
news. And behold, you will be silent and unable to
speak until the day that these things take place, because you did not believe my words, which will be
fulfilled in their time (Luke 1:19-20).*

Sure enough, upon exiting the Temple Zechariah was unable to speak to his friends, thus they
realized that he had seen an angel.

Not long afterwards Elizabeth became preg-
nant. Months later when she delivered a baby boy

she insisted they name him John, which means *"God is gracious"*. When they asked his father Zechariah he likewise confirmed his name was to be John by writing it on a tablet. Then suddenly his tongue was loosed and to the amazement of all who witnessed these events he began praising God and prophesying about his newborn son as follows:

> *Blessed be the Lord God of Israel, for he has visited and redeemed his people and has raised up a horn of salvation for us in the house of his servant David, as he spoke by the mouth of his holy prophets from of old, that we should be saved from our enemies and from the hand of all who hate us; to show the mercy promised to our fathers and to remember his holy covenant, the oath that he swore to our father Abraham, to grant us that we, being delivered from the hand of our enemies, might serve him without fear, in holiness and righteousness before him all our days. And you, child, will be called the prophet of the Most High; for you will go before the Lord to prepare his ways, to give knowledge of salvation to his people in the forgiveness of their sins, because of the tender mercy of our God, whereby the sunrise shall visit us from on high to give light to those who sit in darkness and in the shadow of death, to guide our feet into the way of peace (Luke 1:68-79).*

In these prophetic words of Zechariah we have a remarkable comparison made between John and Jesus. While John is described as the *"prophet of the Most High"*, Jesus is described as the *"Lord"* himself. Thus John is tasked with preparing the way for the promised Messiah who would shine his righteous light on all peoples delivering them from the shadows of darkness.

Fast-forward thirty years; by now John and Jesus were grown men. During this time John had spent a great deal of time in the Judean wilderness preparing for public ministry. Then he made his public appearance by the Jordan River with a simple but compelling message: *"Repent, for the kingdom of heaven is at hand."* He further claimed to be the *"voice in the wilderness"* charged with preparing the way for the Lord. John was something to behold; he wore a garment of camel's hair and a leather belt around his waist reminiscent of ancient prophets like Elijah, and his food was a unique diet of locusts and wild honey.

People from Jerusalem and the surrounding region began to flock to him. Upon confession of their sins, John baptized them in the river, as a sign of their repentance. The ritual of baptism predated John and had by then become a common symbol of purification. For example, anyone who wanted to enter the Temple precincts in Jerusalem, first needed to bathe in a mikvah, where the worshiper was immersed in fresh water. John however was drawing people away from these corrupt religious institutions and urging them to cleanse their hearts in preparation for the imminent arrival of the Messiah.

As word of his message spread, the religious

leaders of the day also came to inquire of John. But when he saw many of the Pharisees and Sadducees coming to his baptism, he had a strong message for them, *"You brood of vipers! Who warned you to flee from the wrath to come? Bear fruit in keeping with repentance. And do not presume to say to yourselves, 'We have Abraham as our father.' Even now the axe is laid to the root of the trees. Every tree therefore that does not bear good fruit is cut down and thrown into the fire" (Matthew 3:7-10).*

Naturally John and his message created quite a stir in Israel. Some wondered if he was the promised Messiah but he emphatically rejected that notion. He said: *"I baptize you with water for repentance, but he who is coming after me is mightier than I, whose sandals I am not worthy to carry. He will baptize you with the Holy Spirit and fire" (Matthew 3:11).* With these words, John made it abundantly clear that he in no way saw himself as a rival or even on the same level as the coming Messiah.

At this time Jesus, who had been living in Nazareth, came to John at the Jordan River asking to be baptized with the rest of the people. Previously, God had made known to John that he would recognize the Messiah when he saw the Spirit of God descending on him like a dove. So when Jesus was baptized, even as he came up from the water, the heavens opened above him, and John saw the Spirit of God descending in the form of a dove and coming to rest on Jesus. Then suddenly a majestic voice from heaven said, *"This is my beloved Son, with whom*

I am well pleased." In this way God made the identity of Jesus imminently clear to all.

In the days that followed John continued to testify to those gathered of all that he had witnessed. When he saw Jesus passing by he further proclaimed: *"Behold, the Lamb of God, who takes away the sin of the world! This is he of whom I said, 'After me comes a man who ranks before me, because he was before me.' I myself did not know him, but for this purpose I came baptizing with water, that he might be revealed to Israel" (John 1:29-31).* John clearly saw Jesus as vastly superior to himself. He also hinted at Christ's ultimate mission by stating that he was the one would save all of mankind by sacrificing himself.

Around this time John was arrested by King Herod Antipas for criticizing his illicit marriage to his brother's wife. During this time Jesus continued his ministry and at one point brought up the subject of John: *"What did you go out into the wilderness to see? A reed shaken by the wind? What then did you go out to see? A man dressed in soft clothing? Behold, those who wear soft clothing are in kings' houses. What then did you go out to see? A prophet? Yes, I tell you, and more than a prophet. This is he of whom it is written, 'Behold, I send my messenger before your face, who will prepare your way before you.' Truly, I say to you, among those born of women there has arisen no one greater than John the Baptist" (Matthew 11:7-11).*

The startling claim that Jesus made regarding John is only surpassed by the comments John previously made about Jesus. Here Jesus made his admiration for John evident to all. He went further to claim that John was more than a prophet. This statement is particularly interesting because John had previously said that he was not worthy to even touch the sandals of Jesus. So if John the Baptist, the greatest prophet, sees Jesus as immeasurably superior to himself then it follows that Jesus is in fact much more than a prophet or great sage. He is, as John stated, the very Son of God.

In the succeeding months John's life came to a tragic end at the hands of Herod and his vindictive wife. Jesus was deeply grieved by the loss of his forerunner and friend. At a later date Jesus' gives John a tremendous tribute in a discussion with the religious leaders. In an effort to discredit him they asked Jesus by what authority he was teaching and preaching to the people. Jesus, astutely responded with another question.

> *I also will ask you one question, and if you tell me the answer, then I also will tell you by what authority I do these things. The baptism of John, from where did it come? From heaven or from man?"* The religious leaders discussed this among themselves, saying, *"If we say, 'From heaven,' he will say to us, 'Why then did you not believe him?' But if we say, 'From man,' we are afraid of the crowd, for they all hold that John was a prophet."* So they answered Jesus, *"We do not know."* And Jesus said to them, *"Neither will I tell you by what authority I do these things (Matthew 21:23-27).*

Now at first glance it may seem that Jesus was being evasive in his answer, but actually he was wanting to highlight their hypocrisy while actually responding to their query. In this interchange it becomes evident that the religious leaders knew that John was inspired by God in his ministry. Jesus, by linking his message and ministry to John's, makes it clear that he operated with the same divine authority that empowered John.

The unique relationship between John and Jesus and their shared mission should cause us to stop and think. On the one hand Jesus is clear that he believes John was commissioned by God to be the forerunner of the Messiah and that as such he was the greatest prophet in history. John, however, in his assessment of Jesus doesn't see himself as worthy to even touch his feet. He famously said of Jesus: *"He must increase but I must decrease."* This alone should challenge any notion we might have of Jesus being simply a prophet. Even though there was no fanfare at his arrival, the one responsible to prepare people's hearts for the Messiah is unequivocal in his praise for Jesus.

THE CRUSHING
OF THE SERPENT

So far we have seen that Jesus, whose coming was predicted long before by the prophets, is himself far above them all. While they were all commissioned by God to pave the way for the Messiah, they were also each keenly aware of their own sinfulness and ultimate need of a Savior. From the outset Jesus is unparalleled in that by being born miraculously from a virgin, he did not inherit the sinful nature passed on from Adam to all mankind. Because of this he is able to take on and ultimately defeat the arch enemy of humanity, that old crafty serpent, Satan, who deceived our ancestors.

After being baptized by John in the Jordan River, the Bible records an epic encounter between Jesus and Satan in the wilderness. Clearly it is no coincidence that Jesus, after being affirmed and anointed as the Messiah by John, begins his ministry career by facing off with the devil himself. In fact it was the Spirit of God who directed him to the wilderness for this very purpose.

Jesus began by fasting forty days and forty nights in preparation for this showdown. Then, when he was physically most vulnerable, the tempter came and said to him, *"If you are the Son of God, command these stones to become loaves of bread."* In what might seem to be a harmless suggestion, Satan was actually enticing Jesus to use his divine powers to satisfy his own physical cravings. But Jesus answered, *"It is written, 'Man shall not live by bread alone, but by every word that comes from the mouth of God.'"* With these words Jesus made it clear that his human needs were in fact subjected to the will of God and that he would not act unilaterally to fulfill his own desires.

Then the devil took him to the holy city Jerusalem and set him on the pinnacle of the Temple and said to him, *"If you are the Son of God, throw yourself down, for it is written, 'He will command his angels concerning you,' and 'On their hands they will bear you up, lest you strike your foot against a stone.'"* Satan here shrewdly quoted the Bible in an attempt to lure Jesus into seeking his own glory. He admittedly recognized Jesus to be the Son of God, but urged him to prove it to the people by performing a miraculous stunt in the Temple precincts, the religious center of the Jewish community. Jesus refused to acquiesce and responded, *"Again it is written, 'You shall not put the Lord your God to the test.'"*

Again, the devil took him to a very high mountain and showed him all the kingdoms of the world and their glory. And he said to him, *"All these I will give you, if you will fall down and worship me."* In his third attempt Satan made it abundantly clear that he knew why Jesus had shown up. He knew that Jesus had come to take back the reins of the Kingdom of earth from the devil. Thus he offered to give it straightway if he would only bow to him. But Jesus said to him, *"Be gone, Satan! For it is written, 'You shall worship the Lord your God and him only shall you serve.'"* So the devil left Jesus alone.

This epic confrontation between Satan and Jesus is reminiscent of the first encounter between the tempter and our ancestors in the Garden of Eden at the dawn of creation. At that time Adam and Eve were entrusted with governing God's good earth. However the moment they gave in to Satan's lies and joined his rebellion against God, they forfeited their right to rule the earth and in fact handed over control to the devil. Ever since then Satan has been in charge, ever-bolstered by ongoing human rebellion against God's will.

However, from the beginning, God had made it clear that he would not allow the serpent to have its way forever. Satan was fully aware of God's promises to send one who would bring his dark regime to an end and regain the rulership of the earth. The echoes of this cosmic spiritual battle can be heard down through history and they come to a head in the life of Jesus.

Unlike the first Adam, Jesus did not fall for the devil's schemes. Satan was fully aware of Jesus' true identity as the Son of God and his mission to retake control of the world, but he hoped to deceive Jesus just like he had deceived Adam and Eve. Jesus, however, proved to be well up to the challenge and he bested Satan at every level. Thus Jesus began the great reconquest of earth.

Throughout the rest of the life and ministry of Jesus we can observe the repercussions of this overarching spiritual battle between God's kingdom and the kingdom of evil. Jesus breaches the dark fortress of Satan and begins to systematically dismantle his reign of terror and shatter the chains that hold people captive to his pernicious lies. Satan for his part mobilizes the religious elite to try to discredit and ultimately destroy Jesus' efforts to wrest the people from his control. This great struggle will later come to a culmination at the cross.

In the meantime, after proving impregnable to Satan's personal attacks, Jesus began his public ministry by preaching to the ever-growing number of people gathering to hear his message: *"The Kingdom of God is at hand!"* When put in the greater context of the epic battle detailed above, these simple words take on a whole new meaning. Jesus was unequivocally heralding the end of Satan's reign of terror and the restoration of God's kingdom to the earth. This further meant that the promised King, the Messiah, was at hand. Naturally this message sent shock waves through the Jewish community, igniting long suppressed hopes as well as latent fears.

If Jesus' message was not remarkable enough, his impeccable character and the fact that he was able to follow it up with an untold number of miracles proving his divine authority, made it clear he was for real. From the beginning of his ministry he healed all who came to him with any number and variety of sicknesses. He further showed absolute authority over nature; he cast out evil spirits and even raised people from the dead. The Bible is replete with examples of his miraculous feats. Here are just a few:

- The Leper - *"When he came down from the mountain, great crowds followed him. And behold, a leper came to him and knelt before him, saying, "Lord, if you will, you can make me clean." And Jesus stretched out his hand and touched him, saying, "I will; be clean." And immediately his leprosy was cleansed"* (Matthew 8:1-3). In the times of Jesus leprosy was a common sight. Those who contract this bacterial infection can experience nerve damage which results in the inability to feel pain and which can lead to loss of body parts due to unnoticed and repeated injuries. In the first century leprosy was one of the most dreaded diseases primarily because no cure was available and also because those infected by this grotesque skin disease were ostracized from society. Since it was deemed highly contagious lepers were required to refrain from public places.

In this case we find a leper venturing out to find Jesus the famed miracle worker. Naturally, everyone was horrified to see a leper approach Jesus. However, Christ went on to scandalize them even further by actually touching this man infected with the deadly disease. He showed not just the power and will to heal him but he further showed the leper compassion like no other. He restored not just his body to health and strength but he also restored his dignity.

- The Paralytic - *"And behold, some people brought to him a paralytic, lying on a bed. And when Jesus saw their faith, he said to the paralytic, "Take heart, my son; your sins are forgiven." And behold, some of the scribes said to themselves, "This man is blaspheming." But Jesus, knowing their thoughts, said, "Why do you think evil in your hearts? For which is easier, to say, 'Your sins are forgiven,' or to say, 'Rise and walk'? But that you may know that the Son of Man has authority on earth to forgive sins" - he then said to the paralytic - "Rise, pick up your bed and go home." And he rose and went home. When the crowds saw it, they were afraid, and they glorified God, who had given such authority to men"* (Matthew 9:2-8). By now it had become commonplace for people to bring every kind of sick people to Jesus; he never failed to deliver. However on this occasion Jesus surprised them by doing more than just healing the paralytic. In fact, before addressing his physical ailment, by speaking to his spiritual condition, Jesus highlighted the real source of all human problems. It is because sin entered the world that we suffer from all sorts of diseases, natural disasters and death. However, when Jesus forgave this man his sins, the onlookers were naturally shocked. They rightly pointed out that no man has the right to forgive another man's sins; that is God's prerogative! And yet Jesus did not back down. In fact he went on to heal the paralytic as proof that he had the right to forgive people's sins. By doing this Jesus made it abundantly clear that he was operating with divine authority.

- A Woman and a Child - *"While he was saying these things to them, behold, a ruler came in and knelt before him, saying, "My daughter has just died, but come and lay your hand on her, and she will live." And Jesus rose and followed him, with his disciples. And behold, a woman who had suffered from a discharge of blood for twelve years came up behind him and touched the fringe of his garment, for she said to herself, "If I only touch his garment, I will be made well." Jesus turned, and seeing her he said, "Take heart, daughter; your faith has made you well." And instantly the woman was made well. And when Jesus came to the ruler's house and saw the flute players and the crowd making a commotion, he said, "Go away, for the girl is not dead but sleeping." And they laughed at him. But when the crowd had been put outside, he went in and took her by the hand, and the girl arose"* (Matthew 9:18-25). In the first century, as in much of the world today, women and children were not treated as equal to men. Yet, Jesus, both in his action and in his teachings, made it clear that all humans are created in the image of God and worthy of equal respect and dignity. Here, Jesus went out of his way to extend grace to a woman who had suffered great dishonor and shame in the eyes of society. Despite the urgency of the situation at hand, he took time to praise her faith. Then he went on to the ruler's house where his daughter lay dead.

Down through human history death has been the most fearsome foe known to man. Yet here Jesus was completely unfazed by death. In fact he acted as if the young girl was merely sleeping and rebuked the group of mourners, forcing them outside. Then he gently took the child by the hand and brought her back to life. Again we can't help but be astonished at the incredible power and authority Jesus embodied.

- The Demonized Boy - *"And someone from the crowd answered him, "Teacher, I brought my son to you, for he has a spirit that makes him mute. And whenever it seizes him, it throws him down, and he foams and grinds his teeth and becomes rigid. So I asked your disciples to cast it out, and they were not able." And he answered them, "O faithless generation, how long am I to be with you? How long am I to bear with you? Bring him to me." And they brought the boy to him. And when the spirit saw him, immediately it convulsed the boy, and he fell on the ground and rolled about, foaming at the mouth. And Jesus asked his father, "How long has this been happening to him?" And he said, "From childhood. And it has often cast him into fire and into water, to destroy him. But if you can do anything, have compassion on us and help us." And Jesus said to him, "'If you can'! All things are possible for one who believes." Immediately the father of the child cried out and said, "I believe; help my unbelief!" And when Jesus saw that a crowd came running together, he rebuked the unclean spirit, saying to it, "You mute and deaf spirit, I command you, come out of him and never enter him again." And after crying out and convulsing him terribly, it came out, and the boy was like a corpse, so that most of them said, "He is dead." But Jesus took him by the hand and lifted him up, and he arose"* (Mark 9:18-27). Most of us have only seen demon-possessed people in movies, and some may doubt that such evil spirits even exist. However, the Bible is clear that Satan has an army of demons at his disposal, whose aim is to prevent us from enjoying a relationship with

God and ultimately destroy as many as possible. Their effect on us can vary from superficial influence to complete control as is evident in this passage.

This was clearly an extreme case. According to the father, the evil spirit had completely take over the boy's faculties and was actively seeking to kill him. The case was so serious that even Jesus' disciples felt powerless. Jesus, however, was completely undaunted by the demon and the immense influence it wielded over the boy. With a simple but authoritative command, he expelled the demon and then helped the boy to his feet.

There were many other occasions when Jesus exorcized sometimes large numbers of demons at once and restored people to sanity. Many times the demons would recognize Jesus as being the Son of God but he ordered them to keep silence as he would not put up with their antics. Clearly they were no match for his divine power and authority. In all this, Jesus was undoing all the evil propagated by Satan and ultimately preparing the way for the Kingdom of God.

The cosmic struggle between Jesus and the devil can be noticed at many crucial points in the life of Jesus. Finally it all came to a climax when Satan orchestrated the crucifixion of Christ. He imagined that he could destroy the Son of God, but he was totally caught off guard by the resurrection three days later. It was then and there that the serpent was vanquished even as it dealt a death blow to the Savior. But the battle is not over yet. Although fatally wounded the serpent now seeks to take down to hell with itself everyone in its reach. Because of the rejection of the Jews, the promised Kingdom was not fully established in Jesus' first coming. Its full realization awaits the return of Christ at which time he will face off one last time with that old serpent.

*

THE RABBI FROM NAZARETH

When Jesus stepped into human history two thousand years ago, he walked into a highly charged scene rife with political tension and social trauma. At that time the Roman Empire governed most of the known world and the small Jewish province, where Jesus was born and raised, was a hot-bed of dissension. The Jews longed for the arrival of the promised Messiah, who they hoped would destroy their oppressors and finally establish their nation as superior to all others. But, in the meantime, they were divided in their response to the Roman occupation. Some joined the Zealots who resorted to guerrilla tactics against the occupying powers. Others decided to work for the Romans by being informants or collecting taxes from their people, while others simply chose to abandon the cities altogether and live monastic lives with fellow pious Jews in the wilderness.

At this time the two dominant religious and political factions in the Jewish community were the Sadducees and the Pharisees. They represented divergent views on how God's people should live under foreign rule. The Sadducees were largely composed of the religious elite from Jerusalem who controlled the Temple precincts. They were known for their liberal policies and loose Biblical interpretation. The Pharisees on the other hand were mainly made up of religious teachers or scribes, who boasted of conservative life-styles and strict interpretations of the Scriptures. While the Sadducees tried to find ways to accommodate their secular rulers, the Pharisees labored to keep the Jewish people bound to the Law of God and untainted by secularism. The question now is, which group did Jesus join? Neither!

Jesus was careful to remain balanced and nonpartisan when it came to the thorny socio-political issues of his day. While he very much agreed with the Pharisees' straight forward interpretation of the Bible, he denounced their failure to practice what they preached. He also rebuked their ethnocentric narrow-mindedness and, like the Sadducees, was much more congenial in his interactions with foreigners. However in the end it was his loving compassion for the disenfranchised, the poor and maligned, that earned him the scorn of both religious parties. Jesus, however, was committed to not taking sides and instead holding the moral high ground even as he gladly stooped to help everyone in need.

When Jesus began his itinerant teaching ministry, he soon attracted the attention of the religious leaders of his day. The fact that he was teaching the people was not unusual, as there were many other rabbis like Jesus roaming the Galilean countryside. But Jesus was markedly different in a number of areas.

The typical rabbi, or religious teacher, sought to gain a large following to boost his career; Jesus however, was not interested in popularity. A rabbi would strive to attract to his circle the best students of the law but Jesus instead chose a group of fishermen and other outcasts to be his disciples. Rabbis would teach their interpretation of God's Law but Jesus spoke with unique authority, claiming to be the *"Lord"* of the Law. Ultimately what really attracted the most attention were the unprecedented amount of miracles that Jesus performed. Not only that, the fact that he gave authority to his rag-tag group of disciples to also perform miracles in his name, broke all the stereotypes. Soon people from far and wide were flocking to him.

The religious leaders of his day couldn't help but admire Jesus. Not only was he a model Jew, who was deeply committed to God's truth, but he also truly loved and wholeheartedly served the people. From the outset Jesus made it clear that he was not coming with a new religion; rather he was on a mission to fulfill God's promises made in the Old Testament. In fact, he claimed to be the very culmination of God's plan of salvation for all nations.

However, as his powerful message, bolstered by his amazing works, began to resonate in the people's hearts, the inevitable happened. The status quo was challenged. The elegant truth of Jesus' teaching coupled with his holy yet humble lifestyle, only served to highlight the establishment's hypocrisy. They became increasingly jealous of him, because the crowds were leaving them for Jesus. Ultimately, it was his shocking personal claims, that created the greatest consternation among his enemies.

Religious leaders of all parties began to see Jesus as a rival and seek opportunities to challenge him. From the beginning, Pharisees did so especially with regard to secondary laws rooted in Jewish legal tradition. The fact is that Jesus never broke the Law of God but he had qualms with the regulations the Pharisees had added to it as a protective layer. He pointed out that these extra laws were often serving as an excuse for disregarding the original intent of God's Word. Furthermore the Pharisees had become so fixated on enforcing these traditions that they were neglecting to practice the actual commands of God. So, although Jesus shared their commitment to Scriptures, he also reserved his greatest condemnation for their hypocritical teachings and life-styles.

One area in which Jesus made a clear break

from the conservative religious group was in his commitment to genuinely love and serve all people. The Pharisees tended to be very nationalistic in outlook, treating all others with disdain. Now if anyone had a reason to be proud and patriotic it would have been Jesus, who as a descendant of David could lay claim to divine precedence. And yet he never evidenced a hint of ethnic chauvinism.

This is best exemplified in his landmark teaching on love: *"You have heard that it was said, 'You shall love your neighbor and hate your enemy.' But I say to you, Love your enemies and pray for those who persecute you, so that you may be sons of your Father who is in heaven. For he makes his sun rise on the evil and on the good, and sends rain on the just and on the unjust"* (Matthew 5:43-45).

Now it is one thing to teach love and equality but quite another thing to truly embody it. While most people admired his egalitarian approach at least in theory, they were nonetheless shocked to find him actually engaging the 'sinners' of his day. On one occasion when the Pharisees found him eating with tax collectors and other "sinners", Jesus responded to their rebuke by chiding them with their own Scriptures: *"Go and learn what this means: 'I desire mercy, and not sacrifice.' For I came not to call the righteous, but sinners."* He was pointing out that, more than any religious sacrifice, God desires genuine compassion for all.

But Jesus went even further; he even embraced the loathed Samaritans. This people group were half-Jews. Centuries before when the northern kingdom of Israel was exiled those who had been left behind intermarried with pagan peoples. This earned them the bitter contempt of their neighboring Jews. The Samaritans went on to develop their own hybrid faith, drawing from Judaism and other pagan rites; thus the Jews avoided them altogether.

Jesus, however, refused to treat them inhumanely. In fact, on one occasion, he stopped at a well near a Samaritan village where he had a remarkable conversation with a woman. Naturally she was shocked he would give her the time of day. In the course of the conversation she perceived that he was a man of God and proceeded challenge his Jewish heritage, to which he responded:

> *"Woman, believe me, the hour is coming when neither on this mountain nor in Jerusalem will you worship the Father. You worship what you do not know; we worship what we know, for salvation is from the Jews. But the hour is coming, and is now here, when the true worshipers will worship the Father in spirit and truth, for the Father is seeking such people to worship him. God is spirit, and those who worship him must worship in spirit and truth."*
>
> *The woman said to him, "I know that Messiah is coming (he who is called Christ). When he comes, he will tell us all things."*
>
> *Jesus said to her, "I who speak to you am he"* (John 4:21-26).

In his response Jesus made it clear that the promised salvation must come through the Jews, the descendants of Abraham. However in doing so he was careful to stress that all peoples are ultimately welcome to approach God, including the Samaritan woman. This was indeed the mission of the Messiah, not just to deliver his own people from oppression but to bring all people back into harmony with God.

As the true identity of Jesus came into focus, people were forced to make a decision about his claims and their commitment to him. The crowds that followed Jesus wanted him to seize the reins of power and sought on several occasions to coerce him into leading a revolt, but Jesus rebuffed their political ambitions for him. The religious leaders for their part, realizing that they were losing the support of the people and jeopardizing their position with the Roman authorities, resorted to slandering Jesus. They went so far as to accuse Jesus of working for the devil. Thus, Jesus chose to focus on his immediate group of followers who had accepted him as the Messiah and pledged their complete allegiance to him.

It was at this time that Jesus allowed them to see for themselves who he really was. He took three of his closest disciples, Peter, James and John, up to a mountain for a spiritual retreat. As he was praying and his disciples dozed, suddenly he was transformed; his face began to shine and his clothing became dazzling white. The startled disciples then saw two men appear and begin talking with Jesus. Somehow they recognized these men to be the renown prophets Moses and Elijah.

As they sat transfixed watching this glorious scene come to an end, Peter said to Jesus, *"Rabbi, it is good that we are here. Let us make three tents, one for you and one for Moses and one for Elijah."* Peter was clearly amazed to see his rabbi on a par with their great prophets and wanted to somehow preserve the moment. However as he was saying these things, a cloud came and overshadowed them. They were gripped by fear. What was going on? Suddenly the booming voice of God rang out from the cloud, saying, *"This is my Son, my Chosen One; listen to him!"*

As Peter and the others sat in stunned silence there was no mistaking the remarkable message they had just received. God himself had made it abundantly clear that Jesus was no mere rabbi or prophet, he was the very Son of God, the promised Messiah. And as such, he deserved their full attention and devotion. Indeed as the cloud dissipated they looked and saw Jesus all alone.

In the succeeding days Jesus, with an ever growing number of followers in tow, began to make his way to Jerusalem to attend the yearly Passover feast. His disciples were hopeful that Jesus would at this time make a move to overthrow the pagan Roman rulers and establish himself as king. Jesus, however, repeatedly chided them about their selfish ambitions and tried to prepare them for a very different outcome. He told them outright that

once in Jerusalem he would be betrayed and crucified. He further predicted that he would rise from
the dead on the third day. The astonished disciples
largely ignored his warnings and kept dreaming of
new positions in Christ's Kingdom.

Upon arrival to Jerusalem Jesus fulfilled yet
another prophecy by riding into the city on a
young donkey. Centuries earlier the prophet Zechariah had portrayed the Messiah as a humble king,
arriving not on a proud white stallion but rather
on the foal of a donkey. By fulfilling this prophecy,
Jesus made it abundantly clear that he was indeed
the long awaited King. His followers were elated.
The religious establishment, however, was enraged.
They knew that this movement, if left unchecked,
would threaten their monopoly on religious power
and incite the wrath of the Roman rulers, whom
they worked so hard to appease. Consequently they
began to oppose Jesus at every step.

At this time Jesus entered the Temple com-
plex, which was designed to be a visible repre-
sentation of God's holy presence on earth. He was
however deeply troubled by what he encountered.
The religious leaders had turned God's house into a
bazaar. Instead of a sacred environment welcoming
worshipers from far and wide, it had effectively become a money making enterprise. When the average villager showed up with his sacrificial lamb,
the priest would more than often reject it out of
hand and demand he purchase another animal from
the local suppliers. These in turn demanded that

they use local currency and would send them to the money changers. After this runaround, the worshiper was all but robbed clean of both his money and his motivation to worship God.

Jesus was incensed by this racket and took it upon himself to make things right. To the great dismay of the religious leaders he drove out the sellers along with their animals and overturned the tables of the money-changers. In the midst of the cacophony he declared: *"It is written, 'My house shall be a house of prayer,' but you have made it a den of robbers."* The leaders knew he was justified in cleansing the Temple but they did not appreciate losing their lucrative source of income. They could also see that he was greatly loved and respected by the people while they were fast losing control of the situation. However, unwilling either to repent of their abuse of power or to abdicate authority to the legitimate Messiah, they decided instead to do away with him.

In the ensuing week, religious leaders of different parties all took Jesus on in debate, questioning his authority and ultimately seeking to disgrace or discredit him in the eyes of the people. Jesus, however, knowing their true motives, deftly navigated the political landmines and proved more than capable to answer all their questions. Even though he confirmed time and again that he was indeed the promised Messiah, they were now bent on his destruction. Finally, Jesus summarized the situation, as he often did, in a clever parable:

57

Hear another parable. There was a master of a house who planted a vineyard and put a fence around it and dug a winepress in it and built a tower and leased it to tenants, and went into another country. When the season for fruit drew near, he sent his servants to the tenants to get his fruit. And the tenants took his servants and beat one, killed another, and stoned another. Again he sent other servants, more than the first. And they did the same to them. Finally he sent his son to them, saying, 'They will respect my son.' But when the tenants saw the son, they said to themselves, 'This is the heir. Come, let us kill him and have his inheritance.' And they took him and threw him out of the vineyard and killed him. When therefore the owner of the vineyard comes, what will he do to those tenants?"

They said to him, "He will put those wretches to a miserable death and let out the vineyard to other tenants who will give him the fruits in their seasons."

Jesus said to them, "Have you never read in the Scriptures: "'The stone that the builders rejected has become the cornerstone; this was the Lord's doing, and it is marvelous in our eyes'? Therefore I tell you, the kingdom of God will be taken away from you and given to a people producing its fruits. And the one who falls on this stone will be broken to pieces; and when it falls on anyone, it will crush him (Matthew 21:33-44).

Notice that Jesus was careful to put the events of his day into the larger context of God's plan of salvation for mankind. Jesus was not surprised by their rejection, as they had likewise rejected all of God's earlier messengers. He further made it abundantly clear that he knew how this story would end. However the real surprise is that he got the religious leaders, who were listening, to unwittingly condemn their own yet future actions. In the final analysis, Jesus made it clear that the Jewish leaders in particular, would be utterly crushed for their rejection of the Messiah but that God's Kingdom would prevail.

THE VICTORY
OF THE CROSS

After the initial debacle at the Temple and the failed attempts to discredit Jesus in the aftermath, the religious leaders were desperate to find a way to exterminate him. But they were also wary of the crowds that hung on his every word. They did not want to be seen as responsible for destroying such a revered rabbi and miracle worker. What could they do? Finally they got the break they were looking for.

Jesus had gathered with his disciples in a friend's home to celebrate the Passover feast. As was customary at that time one of the group would need to volunteer to wash the filth-encrusted feet of the others before they could begin their meal. Naturally each of them had great aspirations in Jesus' forthcoming kingdom and did not want to stoop to the level of a slave. While they waited for someone to acquiesce, they were suddenly surprised to see Jesus coming toward them stripped down to his waist like a servant, carrying a basin of water. He stooped down and began washing each of their feet. Even though some refused at first, Jesus insisted on cleaning each of their grimy feet. All they could do was watch dumbfounded. Once he was finished he returned fully dressed and said the following:

Do you understand what I have done to you? You call me Teacher and Lord, and you are right, for so I am. If I then, your Lord and Teacher, have washed your feet, you also ought to wash one another's feet. For I have given you an example, that you also should do just as I have done to you. Truly, truly, I say to you, a servant is not greater than his master, nor is a messenger greater than the one who sent him. If you know these things, blessed are you if you do them (John 13:12-17).

After this unforgettable lesson in humility, Jesus went on to take some bread, he broke it and passed it around to them all saying: *"Take and eat, this is my body broken for you."* He also took the ceremonial cup of wine and offered it to them all saying: *"This is my blood poured out for the sins of mankind."* Jesus here enshrined these symbols as a vivid picture and reminder of his sacrificial death for all generations to come. None of what was about to happen was an accident. Neither was Jesus seeking to be a martyr; rather, just as John had predicted, he was offering himself as the Lamb of God for mankind. He then added: "*The hand of the one who will betray me is with mine at this table.*"

Even though the disciples may not have immediately understood the gravity of what Jesus had told them, his final words about one of them betraying him ignited a firestorm. They were soon on a witch-hunt seeking the culprit, but none of them seems to have suspected Judas Iscariot, the treasurer of the group. Jesus, however, privately signaled to him after which he promptly left the room incognito. Evidently, Judas had already spoken to the religious leaders and had received thirty pieces of silver in return for delivering Jesus to them.

How could one of Jesus' own disciples betray him? A few days earlier Jesus and his disciples had gathered for a meal in the home of Lazarus who he had raised from the dead. Suddenly Lazarus' sister, Mary, appeared with a very expensive perfume in hand and poured it out over Jesus' feet, then she wiped them with her hair. It was a scandalous act of pure devotion. At that time, Judas in particular was incensed, decrying the extravagant waste of such a precious resource. Jesus, however, rose to the woman's defense, praising her for recognizing his true identity and for perceiving his forthcoming sacrifice. This was the final straw for Judas, who realized all his hopes of financial success in the cause of Jesus were in vain.

Now, after leaving the Passover meal, under the cover of darkness, he went to the chief leaders of the people. He knew that after the meal Jesus and his disciples would retreat to the Garden of Gethsemane where they often met for prayer. This was a quiet place just outside the city walls, a perfect place to arrest Jesus without causing a ruckus. When he divulged this to the leaders they hurriedly arranged for a cohort of soldiers to go with him to arrest Jesus in the garden.

None of these developments were a surprise to Jesus. After dinner, he went forward with his usual ritual of going to the olive tree grove named Gethsemane for prayer. Once there he urged his disciples to pray with him, as he was feeling overwhelmed by the tremendous burden of taking on the sins of all mankind. After a time of intense prayer he returned to find his disciples fast asleep. He woke them up saying, *"The time is at hand, the son of man is being delivered into the hands of sinners. Let's go! My betrayer is here."*

While he was still speaking, Judas came, with him a large group of men armed with swords and clubs. Now he had given them a sign, saying, *"The one I kiss is the man; seize him."* So he came up to Jesus for the traditional greeting and kissed him. Jesus said to him, *"Friend, do what you came to do."* Then they came up and arrested Jesus. At that moment Peter impulsively drew his sword and struck the servant of the high priest, managing to cut off his ear. But Jesus said to him, *"Put your sword back into its place. For all who take the sword will perish by the sword. Do you think that I cannot appeal to my Father, and he will at once send me more than twelve legions of angels? But how then should the Scriptures be fulfilled, that it must be so?"*

This was undeniably one of the most unusual arrests in human history. Jesus could have easily prevented this confrontation. Likewise, once apprehended he could have easily sprung himself free by some miraculous means. At least he could have allowed his disciples to fight for him. However, he adamantly rebuffed any such efforts on his behalf, insisting instead that all of these things must take place to fulfill God's plan of salvation as outlined in the Scriptures. Indeed, as chaotic as it may have seemed, everything had been carefully choreographed long ago by God himself. Likewise, as predicted by the prophets, his stunned disciples ran away leaving Jesus all alone.

Then those who had seized Jesus brought him to Caiaphas, the high priest of the Jewish religious council. As the other members of the council gathered they were desperately seeking false testimony against Jesus that they might put him to death, but they found none, even though many false witnesses came forward.

Finally, the high priest stood up and said, *"Have you no answer to make? What is it that these men testify against you?"* But Jesus remained silent. Then the high priest said to him, *"I adjure you by the living God, tell us if you are the Christ, the Son of God."* Now this was the real crux of the matter. Jesus had committed no crime. However the fact that he claimed to be the promised Messiah seemed to those who disbelieved him to be a heinous lie on a par with treason.

Jesus said to him, *"You have said so yourself. I tell you, from now on you will see the Son of Man seated at the right hand of God and coming on the clouds of heaven."* Jesus not only responded affirmatively, but he went further to assert that one day each of them would have to stand judgement before his throne.

Beside himself with anger, the high priest tore his robes and shouted, *"He has uttered blasphemy. What further witnesses do we need? You have now heard his blasphemy. What is your judgment?"* They all answered, *"He deserves death."* Then they began to physically abuse Jesus whose only crime had been standing for the truth.

Getting Jesus condemned in their kangaroo court was the easy part; getting him killed would be harder, because he was beloved by the people. The religious leaders needed to pin the blame for his death on someone else. So, after subjecting Jesus to further abuse, early in the morning they approached the official residence of the Roman governor Pilate.

Under normal circumstances Pilate would relish any opportunity to have yet another Jew exterminated. However, upon hearing the charges brought against Jesus and questioning him of his own accord, he quickly realized the farce playing out before him. Ironically, the Roman governor began to do all in his power to deliver Jesus from the chief priest's hands. Eventually he was strong-armed into condemning Jesus to be crucified when the Jewish leaders threatened to file a complaint about him to the Roman emperor himself.

In all this Jesus again remained silent and refused to raise a finger in his own defense. After being brutally whipped by the Roman soldiers he was forced to carry his own cross through the streets of Jerusalem in utter humiliation. When he finally arrived to a small hill called 'The Skull', on the outskirts of the city, he was brutally nailed—hands and feet—to a wooden cross and then propped upright between two other criminals for all in the city to jeer at him. And yet even as he endured the agony of the spikes piercing his flesh Jesus cried out: *"Father forgive them for know not what they do."*

The excruciating pain a person endured as he or she fought for every breath while hanging on crude nails driven into a Roman cross, was only exacerbated by the deep shame one felt from being publicly disgraced in the eyes of all the people. As Jesus endured the ignominy of crucifixion, his mother and a handful of other close relatives looked on in utter dejection. Some of the bystanders shouted out, *"If you are the Son of God, come down from the cross."* So also the chief priests, with the religious leaders, mocked him, saying, *"He saved others; he cannot save himself. He is the King of Israel; let him come down now from the cross, and we will believe in him. He trusts in God; let God deliver him now, if he desires him. For he said, 'I am the Son of God.'"* The criminals who were crucified next to him also reviled him in the same way. Little did they realize that it was in order to save mankind that he refused to save himself.

At around noontime, suddenly the land was engulfed in a palpable darkness which lasted for three hours. After the black blanket lifted, Jesus cried out the most perplexing words, *"My God, my God why have you forsaken me!"* Those around the cross who heard him were likewise perplexed and made light of his agony. What did he mean? These words were actually a direct quote from the first line of Psalm 22 where King David, roughly a thousand years earlier, spoke of the coming Messiah's suffering in gruesome detail. In the Psalm David went on to paint a vivid picture of Jesus' final moments:

> *I am poured out like water, and all my bones are out of joint; my heart is like wax; it is melted within my breast; my strength is dried up like a potsherd, and my tongue sticks to my jaws; you lay me in the dust of death. For dogs encompass me; a company of evildoers encircles me; they have pierced my hands and feet, I can count all my bones, they stare and gloat over me; they divide my garments among them, and for my clothing they cast lots* (Psalm 22:14-18).

These words not only aptly describe the raw emotions and unspeakable horror Jesus endured on the cross but they also predict with amazing precision the details of crucifixion centuries before such a form of capital punishment was even invented. In quoting this passage Jesus was giving his onlookers a bold clue as to what was taking place on the cross, namely, Jesus was fulfilling the prophecies of the Messiah written in their Scriptures. None of this was by chance. The prophets had foretold the sacrificial death of the Messiah long ago.

Soon afterwards Jesus again raised his voice saying, *"It is finished! Father into your hands I commit my spirit."* With these words Jesus made it clear that he had completed the mission he had been sent to accomplish; he had indeed paid for the sins of the world.

As his lifeless body fell limp on the cross the otherwise pagan Roman centurion was so moved by the whole ordeal that he said in amazement, *"Surely this man was the Son of God."* At that moment there was a great earthquake and the other bystanders quickly scattered in fear of further divine repercussion. The close relatives and friends of Jesus lingered on, however, trying to grapple with their own profound sorrow and wondering at all they had witnessed.

Because the Passover festivities was due to start that evening, the religious leaders were eager to put this crisis behind them, so they urged Pilate to have Jesus taken down before sunset. Normally a victim of crucifixion might languish in suffering for days and once dead be thrown into a shallow mass grave. Jesus however, had suffered more than normal and thus expired earlier than expected. His poor family had no means to offer him a proper burial. Right then a secret and rather wealthy follower of Jesus, Joseph of Arimathea, approached them offering to have Jesus placed in his new tomb hewn from the rock nearby. So it was that Jesus, once pronounced dead, was lowered from the cross, hurriedly bound in linen cloths with some aromatic spices, as is the burial custom of the Jews, then placed in a sealed cave.

When the followers of Jesus finally regathered they were overwhelmed with grief. They had had such high hopes for a future with Jesus ruling the promised Kingdom. Now their hopes and dreams lay buried in the grave. The fact that Jesus had made no effort to defend or deliver himself and had refused their attempts to fight for him only added to their consternation. It almost seemed like he wanted to die. But why?

* * *

On the third day, early in the morning, the women returned to the tomb to finish the task of embalming the body and properly burying Jesus. However upon arrival they saw that the stone covering the entrance to the tomb had been cast aside. Peering inside hesitantly they were greeted by two angels who said, *"Why do you seek the living among the dead? He is not here, but has risen. Remember how he told you, while he was still in Galilee, that* the Son of Man must be delivered into the hands of sinful men and be crucified and on the third day rise." Shocked out of their minds, the women hurried back to the disciples to deliver the unbelievable news.

The disciples were likewise stunned by this latest development and afraid that the authorities might blame them for what was certainly a grave robbery. That evening as they were all gathered discussing their options, Jesus suddenly stood in their midst saying, "Peace be with you." His followers initially shrank back thinking they were seeing a ghost to which Jesus responded, "Why are you troubled, and why do doubts arise in your hearts? See my hands and my feet, that it is I myself. Touch me, and see. For a spirit does not have flesh and bones as you see that I have." Jesus went on to eat a piece of fish that they gave him as proof that he was really alive. Only then did their doubts begin to melt away and their hearts fill with inexpressible joy and wonder.

Then Jesus continued, "These were my words that I spoke to you while I was still with you, that everything written about me in the Law of Moses and the Prophets and the Psalms must be fulfilled." Then he opened their minds to understand the Scriptures, and said to them, "Thus it is written, that the Christ should suffer and on the third day rise from the dead, and that repentance for the forgiveness of sins should be proclaimed in his name to all nations, beginning from Jerusalem. You are witnesses of these things. And behold, I am sending the promise of my

Father, the Holy Spirit upon you. But stay in the city until you are clothed with power from on high" (Luke 24:46-49).

So it was that Jesus defeated death by dying on the cross and rose victorious from the grave. He singlehandedly took all the weight of human sin and guilt upon himself and paid our eternal debt with his own blood. In doing so he forged a way of salvation from sin and death for all mankind.

THE COMING
OF THE KING

As Jesus had stressed repeatedly, the things he endured were no accident. All of these were part of a greater plan designed before time by God to bring salvation to all mankind. Just as the prophets had predicted long before, Jesus had offered his perfect life as a payment for the sin of men and women of all time. He had also succeeded in crushing the head of that conniving serpent, Satan, and thus offered those who would believe in him ultimate freedom from his evil domain. So it is that any who upon recognition of their sinful condition put their full trust in Jesus for their eternal salvation, are granted full forgiveness by God.

However, some questions still loom large; what about the promised Kingdom? Jesus may have obtained salvation for our souls but when will this sad world be saved from the curse of sin and be restored to all that God originally intended? Yes, the devil was crushed but why is he still on the loose and why does evil still run rampant? When will Jesus bring the fullness of his Kingdom to earth?

After rising unexpectedly from the grave, Jesus gave ample proof of his victory to his disciples in the succeeding forty days he spent with them. After getting over the initial shock of his resurrection, they also began to wonder: What about the Kingdom? To this Jesus answered, *"It is not for you to know times or seasons that the Father has fixed by his own authority. But you will receive power when the Holy Spirit has come upon you, and you will be my witnesses in Jerusalem and in all Judea and Samaria, and to the end of the earth."* Clearly the Kingdom was still on, but there as a task to accomplish in the meantime, this good news must be spread to all peoples.

Before his death, Jesus had often spoken of the "Helper" which he would send to empower them in his absence. This was not some other prophet, because no one could ever come and do any more than Jesus had already accomplished. In fact, he made it clear that he was speaking of a spiritual being who would indwell each of them. He had assured them that they would not be left alone in the monumental task of spreading this good news to the nations, but that he would in fact be leading them from heaven and operating within them in the form of the Holy Spirit.

So it was that as Jesus met with his disciples for a final farewell on the Mount of Olives, he was suddenly lifted into the clouds and soon disappeared from their sight. While they were still gazing into heaven, suddenly, two angels stood by them in white robes, and said, *"Men of Galilee, why do you stand looking into heaven? This Jesus, who was taken up from you into heaven, will come in the same way as you saw him go into heaven."* Encouraged by this promise that Jesus would indeed return, the disciples went back to Jerusalem to await the arrival of the promised Holy Spirit.

In the latter part of his ministry Jesus had often spoken to his disciples about his second coming. Especially when leaders of his own people, the Jews, outright rejected him as their Messiah he made it clear that the fulfillment of God's promised Kingdom would be postponed. In fact he stated that until this nation, the chosen people of God who had received all the promises, repented and welcomed him back, they would not be seeing him again. Only then would Christ return to fully establish his Kingdom on earth so that all peoples and nations would finally be brought back into harmony with God.

On one occasion his disciples had specifically asked Jesus to describe in detail the events surrounding his second coming. Jesus responded with a series of stark warnings:

> *See that no one leads you astray. For many will come in my name, saying, 'I am the Christ,' and they will lead many astray. And you will hear of wars and rumors of wars. See that you are not alarmed, for this*

must take place, but the end is not yet. For nation will rise against nation, and kingdom against kingdom, and there will be famines and earthquakes in various places. All these are but the beginning of the birth pains. "Then they will deliver you up to tribulation and put you to death, and you will be hated by all nations for my name's sake. And then many will fall away and betray one another and hate one another. And many false prophets will arise and lead many astray. And because lawlessness will be increased, the love of many will grow cold. But the one who endures to the end will be saved. And this gospel of the Kingdom will be proclaimed throughout the whole world as a testimony to all nations, and then the end will come (Matthew 24:4-14).

In his discourse on the end times, Jesus first warned his disciples about the proliferation of false prophets. Since the time of Jesus there have been many who have tried to take his place or pretended to be some final prophet. From the outset Jesus was clear that these would be impostors seeking only to promote themselves and deceive people. Clearly we are not to expect any other Savior aside from Jesus. Since he already defeated death and provided eternal life for all mankind, what more could anyone else offer us?

Regarding the last days Jesus also warned of great conflagrations and catastrophes that would shake the earth to its core. Now, wars and earthquakes are nothing new; how will this be different?

Jesus likened these to birth pangs which become more frequent and more painful as the moment of birth approaches. In a similar way we can expect the interval between cataclysmic events linked to the end times to shorten dramatically even as they increase in intensity. The world will find itself suddenly overwhelmed by disasters right and left. But when the pangs reach their climax they will give way to that long-awaited moment of inexpressible joy, the return of Jesus Christ.

During the years leading up to the return of Jesus to earth, Jesus warned that his people will also suffer intense persecution and even martyrdom. True believers will be ostracized and vilified as they have been for much of the last two millennia. But even in the midst of these trying times the good news of Jesus will finally reach to every corner of the earth and an unprecedented spiritual revival will sweep the globe. In a way it will indeed be the "best of times and the worst of times."

In many related passages the Bible warns of a great world leader who will rise to power during this last phase of human history. Armed with a charming personality and a monstrous ego he will succeed in deceiving many people into believing that he is, in fact, the end times' savior of mankind. He will rise to political power at the helm of a ten-nation coalition which in turn will promise to lay the groundwork for peace in the Middle East. After the initial success of his peace initiative, everything will begin to unravel and the world will be plunged into war, famine and death.

This final world leader, otherwise known as the Antichrist, will later enter the rebuilt Temple of the Jews in Jerusalem and surprise everyone by claiming to be divine and demanding that all worship him. He will boastfully rail against the one true God, persecute his people and ultimately desecrate God's house. In this way his true face will be unmasked and his allegiance to Satan made evident to all who are willing to acknowledge it.

He will be joined by another who claims to be a prophet and performs signs and wonders in order to convince people to worship the great leader. Together they will set up a reign of terror in which only those who pledge allegiance to him will be allowed a measure of freedom. Finally they will muster the armies of their allies for a final attack on Jerusalem. However, in this final battle of Armageddon, they will meet their rightful end.

During these final chaotic months God will likewise be raining down on earth his final judgments. After centuries of injustice and unchecked violence perpetrated on innocent lives, God will finally pour out his long awaited wrath. Horrendous plagues will be unleashed: seas and rivers will turn to blood, the sun will scorch the earth, later utter darkness will engulf the planet even as evil spirits are let loose to raise havoc. The earth will be racked with such powerful earthquakes that mountains will disintegrate even as whole islands are swallowed up by the sea.

At this crucial moment in history, even as they face yet another holocaust, the Jewish nation, the people of Jesus, will finally and fully recognize him as their long awaited Messiah. They will mourn for him as one mourns for the loss of an only son. This national repentance will then trigger the return of their Savior, the King of Kings. Jesus himself described the final scene like this:

> *Immediately after the tribulation of those days the sun will be darkened, and the moon will not give its light, and the stars will fall from heaven, and the powers of the heavens will be shaken. Then will appear in heaven the sign of the Son of Man, and then all the tribes of the earth will mourn, and they will see the Son of Man coming on the clouds of heaven with power and great glory. And he will send out his angels with a loud trumpet call, and they will gather his elect from the four winds, from one end of heaven to the other* (Matthew 24:29-31).

At the height of all these military campaigns and cataclysmic events Jesus will appear for all the world to see, just as he promised. First of all he will gather all his followers to himself. Included in this will be the resurrection of all believers who will then join Jesus in the clouds. Then he will proceed to earth to intervene in the battle raging in Jerusalem. His feet will touch down on the Mount of Olives from where he will singlehandedly wage war on all the armies gathered to destroy his people. As they try to flee in panic he will destroy them with the word of his mouth. He will further apprehend the last world leader and his false prophet and banish them to the fires of hell. Finally he will seize that old serpent the devil and condemn him to eternal punishment in hell.

In this way the kingdom of this world will finally be restored to its rightful owner. Jesus will finally sit on the throne of his ancestor King David in the new world capital Jerusalem. He will be the unrivaled ruler of the whole world. After his enemies are purged, the rest of mankind will be allowed to live in peace and harmony in a renewed earth under Christ's gracious rule. Resurrected believers will likewise reign with Jesus in this Kingdom that will last one thousand years.

This will be an unparalleled time of peace and prosperity in which the world will largely be restored to its pre-fall condition. The Bible speaks of the lion and the lamb lying together in complete tranquility. The weapons of warfare will be turned into implements for farming as the earth is once again restored to its original fertility. All nations will pay homage to the Son of God who reigns with absolute righteousness from Jerusalem.

At the end of the millennium, this earth along with the vestiges of sin and death, will finally be relegated to history, as God welcomes all his people into their new and eternal home. In the new heaven and earth there will no longer be any signs of evil. Sorrow and pain will be forever replaced with unbridled joy and love. Our new residence will be the gold-studded New Jerusalem. But all the inexpressible glories of heaven aside, the greatest joy of our final dwelling place will be the fact that we will live forever in the very presence of God. That is in fact the ultimate purpose of our existence.

The final book of the New Testament, the Revelation, reveals in greater detail much of what was only summarized above. Most importantly in this final chapter of the Bible, Jesus himself appears to his apostle John urging all believers to be ready for his imminent return: *"Behold, I am coming soon, bringing my recompense with me, to repay each one for what he has done. I am the Alpha and the Omega, the first and the last, the beginning and the end"* (Revelation 20:12-13).

People may have all manner of diverse opinions about Jesus, however, when we take to heart his own words we are forced to recognize his true identity. Not only was he the promised one who fulfilled every prophecy made of him, he was also the only perfect man to ever live. As such he not only exemplified the most perfect life in service to others but he ultimately gladly laid it down as a sacrifice for all mankind. The fact that he rose again victorious over death on the third day, is proof positive that the salvation he offers is indeed real and available to all mankind. This same Jesus is alive now and will one day return in glory to welcome all who have trusted in him to join him in his Kingdom. From beginning to end Jesus is the answer. Peter said it best when he said, *"There is salvation in no one else, for there is no other name under heaven given among men by which we must be saved"* (Acts 4:12).

A FINAL WORD

Now that you have met the real Jesus you have an important choice to make. It would be all too tempting to just brush aside all you've read about this remarkable individual as mere legendary tales or sheer religious propaganda. But the fact remains that the Biblical narrative has been confirmed many times over by historians and archeologists alike. H.G. Wells, the renowned English writer, famously admitted, "I am a historian, I am not a believer, but I must confess as a historian that this penniless preacher from Nazareth is irrevocably the very center of history. Jesus Christ is easily the most dominant figure in all history."

Each of us must come to terms with Jesus. It is all too easy and maybe excusable for those not fully aware of the facts to claim that he was just a godly man or a great prophet. But for you who have now come to know this unique man up close, that is no longer an option. C.S. Lewis, one of the brightest minds from the previous century, a former atheist converted to Christ, warned about apathy towards this very question:

> "A man who was merely a man and said the sort of things Jesus said would not be a great moral teacher. He would either be a lunatic – on a level with the man who says he is a poached egg – or else he would be the devil of Hell. You must make your choice. Either this man was, and is, the Son of God; or else a madman or something worse. You can shut him up for a fool, you can spit at him and kill him as a demon; or you can fall at his feet and call him Lord and God. But let us not come with any patronizing nonsense about his being a great human teacher. He has not left that open to us. He did not intend to" (Mere Christianity).

Soon after the resurrection of Jesus, a passionate Jewish student of the law named Saul, began to hear the incredible reports about the rabbi from Nazareth. His religious sensibilities were incensed by such reports and even more so by the growing number of Jews flocking to this new found faith. He was particularly offended by Jesus' followers claiming that he was not only the promised Messiah but the Lord God himself. This was sacrilegious! He tried to reason with them but found their arguments rooted in the Old Testament all too persuasive. He was sure they were wrong about Jesus; he simply could not prove it. There must be another way, this heresy must be expunged from the community.

Saul soon came to believe that violence was the only means to stop this "heretical" movement. After losing yet another debate, he arranged for his Christian rival to be arrested on false charges of blasphemy. After hearing more of his foe's arguments in court, the religious leaders were equally incensed by Stephen's testimony of Jesus, so much so that they rushed him out of the city to stone him.

From then on Saul's fury against the followers of Jesus knew no bounds. He began to go house to house hunting down the disciples of Jesus. Those he captured were dragged off to prison, those charged were executed. In a short time the followers of Jesus had scattered and Saul had become the new hero of the Jewish community.

But this was not enough. Saul heard that some of the disciples had gathered in Damascus and were poisoning the minds of the Jews there. So he pressed the high priest for letters of safe passage to Damascus so he could root out the heretics there as well. Later as he approached that city, suddenly a light from heaven shone around him. Falling to the ground, he heard a voice saying to him, *"Saul, Saul, why are you persecuting me?"* Stunned, Saul responded, *'Who are you?'* The voice answered, *'I am Jesus whom you are persecuting. But rise and stand upon your feet, for I have appeared to you for this purpose, to appoint you as a servant and witness to the things in which you have seen me and to those in which*

I will appear to you, delivering you from your people and from the Gentiles, to whom I am sending you to open their eyes, so that they may turn from darkness to light and from the power of Satan to God, that they may receive forgiveness of sins and a place among those who are sanctified by faith in me' (Acts 26:14-18).

The rest is truly history. In time, Saul the chief antagonist of Christianity became Paul the chosen apostle. The man dedicated to destroying the followers of Jesus became the greatest defender of the faith. The madman became a missionary taking the message of Jesus all over the Roman Empire. The letters he penned became the well-spring of Christian theology.

Years later, confined to a dank Roman dungeon awaiting martyrdom, the apostle Paul penned his last letter to his follower and friend Timothy, in which he said,

Remember Jesus Christ, risen from the dead, the off-spring of David, as preached in my gospel, for which I am suffering, bound with chains as a criminal. But the word of God is not bound! Therefore I endure everything for the sake of the elect, that they also may obtain the salvation that is in Christ Jesus with eternal glory (2.Timothy 2:8-10).

The fact is that no one has ever been able to stifle this good news of Jesus. This tremendous message of eternal salvation for all mankind has echoed down through the corridors of time finding voice in some of the most unlikely people from Saul of Tarsus to C.S. Lewis of Oxford.

The truth of Jesus' claims have been challenged again and again but they still stand undaunted, inviting all who will hear: *"I am the resurrection and the life. Whoever believes in me, though he die, yet shall he live,"* No mere human or great prophet would dare to say such words. Jesus either really meant what he said or he means nothing at all. He is either God in human flesh or he is merely another imposter.

If you choose to believe the message of the Bible and take Jesus at his word, then you will accept that he is indeed *"the way, the truth and the life."* This means that all he promises about forgiveness from sins, freedom from Satan and victory over death are indeed true! They are true for you too. Jesus is all you have ever wanted, all you have ever hoped for. He is in fact the answer to all your questions and the only way to an abundant life now and forever. He is all you need, Jesus alone!

EPILOGUE

Once you have come to accept the real Jesus as Lord of your life then you simply start to follow him in loving obedience. Like Peter and Paul you also become a disciple of the Messiah and learn to walk in his footsteps. Jesus said, *"If you love me, you will keep my commandments."*

It is impossible for us to accomplish this alone. But Jesus promised to be with his disciples every step of the way, *"I will not leave you as orphans; I will come to you... Because I live, you also will live. In that day you will know that I am in my Father, and you in me, and I in you. Whoever has my commandments and keeps them, he it is who loves me. And he who loves me will be loved by my Father, and I will love him and manifest myself to him."*

The best way to know God's commandments is to read and study his Word, the Bible, asking him to reveal his truth to you. As he promised, each of us who trusts in him for salvation receives the Holy Spirit, who indwells us and begins the process of transformation in us. The Spirit of Jesus does indeed lead us into all truth and helps us draw ever closer to God until the day of his glorious appearing and the restoration of all things.

ACKNOWLEDGE-MENT

I am especially grateful to the many individuals and churches that have prayerfully supported our family in our years of ministry in the Middle East. Although not always visible to the naked eye, God is doing amazing things around the world. He promised to build his church and nothing will stop him from doing so. I am also particularly humbled by the loving support of my wife Sarah in this long journey together. Thank you.

ABOUT THE AUTHOR

Jerry Mattix

Jerry and his wife Sarah have served as ambassadors of Jesus Christ in the Middle East for over 20 years. God has blessed them with three natural children and many more spiritual children. Their heart's desire is to make disciples of all nations just as the Lord Jesus commanded.

BOOKS BY THIS AUTHOR

Dear Muslim Friend

Dear Muslim Friend seeks to answer the basic questions Muslims are commonly asking about Christianity. These include:

Hasn't the Bible been changed?
How could Jesus be the Son of God?
Didn't someone else die on the cross instead of Jesus?
Why do Christians not accept the prophet Mohammed?

Dear Skeptic Friend

Dear Skeptic Friend strives to present logical answers to the big questions of life based both on the biblical narrative and verifiable scientific data. It addresses questions like:

Can belief in God stand the test of logic and science?

If God exists, how can he allow so much evil in the world?

How can we possibly trust the Bible to be reliable?

What about all the alleged contradictions in the Bible?

Made in the USA
Columbia, SC
26 April 2025